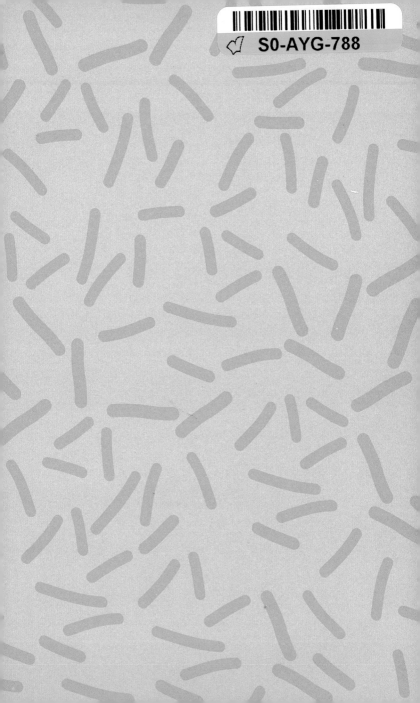

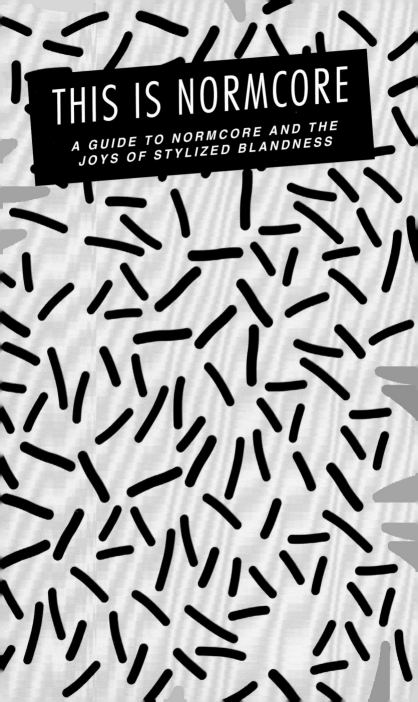

THIS IS NORMCORE

A GUIDE TO NORMCORE AND THE JOYS OF STYLIZED BLANDNESS

THIS IS NORMCORE

A GUIDE TO NORMCORE AND THE JOYS OF STYLIZED BLANDNESS

JO HOARE

DOG 'n' BONE

Published in 2015 by Dog 'n' Bone Books
An imprint of Ryland Peters & Small Ltd
20–21 Jockey's Fields   341 E 116th St
London WC1R 4BW   New York, NY 10029

www.rylandpeters.com

10 9 8 7 6 5 4 3 2 1

Text © Jo Hoare
Design and illustration © Dog 'n' Bone Books 2015

A CIP catalog record for this book is available from
the Library of Congress and the British Library.

ISBN: 978 1 909313 59 0

Printed in China

Editor: Jennifer Jahn
Designer: Eoghan O'Brien
Illustrator: Paul Parker

CONTENTS

INTRODUCTION:

WHAT IS NORMCORE?

YOU MAY HAVE NOTICED THE SUDDEN UBIQUITY OF TERRIBLE FASHION TRENDS FROM THE NINETIES, OR THE FACT THAT KIDS ARE DRESSING LIKE RETIRED ACCOUNTANTS ON A CRUISE TRIP TO BELGIUM. BUT WHY SHOULD WE CARE?

All good things must come to an end. And so must all crap things—which is why we're about to break the news to you that the age of the hipster is over. Oh yes, was it the second Katy Perry got drainbow hair? The exact point Rob Kardashian premiered a sleeve? Or just when the number of men sporting Victorian poisoner-inspired beards outnumbered those who didn't? The time of death of the hipster is somewhat hazy, but we can definitely pronounce the movement deceased.

Before you rejoice too much and revel in the thought of freedom to dress in a way that doesn't let anyone within a visual radius instantly know that you're a douchebag, beware of the power vacuum that's been left behind, for in the wake of the hipster comes something that could be even more annoying. Ladies and Gentlemen, ready yourself for **Normcore**...

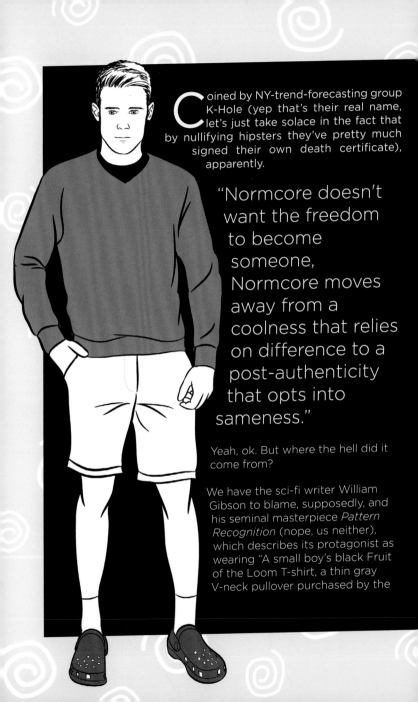

Coined by NY-trend-forecasting group K-Hole (yep that's their real name, let's just take solace in the fact that by nullifying hipsters they've pretty much signed their own death certificate), apparently.

"Normcore doesn't want the freedom to become someone, Normcore moves away from a coolness that relies on difference to a post-authenticity that opts into sameness."

Yeah, ok. But where the hell did it come from?

We have the sci-fi writer William Gibson to blame, supposedly, and his seminal masterpiece *Pattern Recognition* (nope, us neither), which describes its protagonist as wearing "A small boy's black Fruit of the Loom T-shirt, a thin gray V-neck pullover purchased by the

half-dozen from a supplier to the New England prep schools, and a new and oversized pair of black 501's, every trademark carefully removed," and it's from this that those K-Hole crazy kids dreamt up the whole phenomenon. So nothing to do with the fact that everyone's a bit broke and can't really be bothered to buy new clothes then? Course not. If all it takes to prophesy an entire new fashion genre is half a paragraph in an old paperback, let's just be thankful that no one at K-Hole had a Fifty Shades of Grey habit.

So far, so first-year college assignment (with a pass grade at best). Take away the jargon and what does it really mean? Well, dressing like your dad. Or your mom. Or someone who works in Walmart. Or a middle-aged tourist playing mini golf. Still haven't got it? Think of yourself as an urban chameleon or, if that sounds too dickish, someone who doesn't want to be picked on in the front row of a stand-up comedy show. Basically, you need to be as bland and anonymous as possible while still (and this is the tricky bit, and why you need a 64-page guide) standing out as an example of high fashion. Can such a thing really be possible? Read on...

CHAPTER ONE:

NORMSTYLE

CARGO PANTS

Normcore is very much a consciously no-hassle trend (with no hassle meaning actually quite a lot of hassle, really, enough to have a whole book about it anyway), and nothing says "I like to avoid hassle" like ditching the ball-and-chain-esque handbag/manbag. You don't want the shackles of such a superfluous bit of fashion frippery while you're living your busy life of doing everyday things like drinking tea, going on cultural city breaks, or taking a Sunday stroll along the river.

But hang on, where are you going to put the bits you bought at the supermarket? After all, you're too eco-conscious to be using the shop's plastic bags. And you'd really like to take an umbrella out with you tonight in case it rains on the way home from your knitting circle, but as you're not willing to give up your hands-free life for anyone, you're just going to have to struggle on, right? Wrong! Meet the cargo pants (note that in certain circles and retail venues you may see these referred to as combat pants, but do not under any circumstances purchase anything in camouflage print, especially not anything in the Desert Storm family): with their handy multi-pockets you never need be without personal storage again. Is it really as easy as that, though?

Of course it isn't, and the rules around the wear of this item must be fully committed to memory before any kind of purchase is made. Firstly, do not play fast and loose with pocket numbers. Four is best practice: two standard pockets, plus two mid-thigh; anything more than that strays into jazzy survival-expert territory. Also, do not be tempted to think you can double your wear and snap up a pair of Oscar Pistorius cargo pants—i.e. with a removable lower leg. It might look practical to be able to zip on and off and create yourself a handy pair of shorts, but it's not Normcore.

THE SLIDER

On the whole, anything too designer-y should scare off the typical Normcorer. Where mass-produced and mall-available garments rule, spending a whole month's rent on any one item is way too "try hard" for the consciously unconscious Normcore shopper. Only a few items have managed to break through this—the most notable being Isabel Marant pool sliders. Despite their $500 price tag, these shoes from her spring/summer 2014 collection sold out almost instantly and appeared on more blogs than One Direction homoerotic fan fiction.

These are essentially a slightly swankier version of the plastic slippers 1980s lifeguards wore to avoid warts and pubic hairballs at public swimming pools, and Normcore has spawned a thousand copies—including the exact ones 1980s lifeguards used to wear. In lurid neon with ironic wave motifs, Nike and Adidas have made a fortune from their clammy-but-verruca-free-footed, slider-wearing Normcore emperors, all proudly showing off their new clothes. Managing to be almost as uncomfortable as they are unattractive, sliders have a satisfying amount of uselessness, being totally impractical to wear anywhere that is chlorine free. But don't let that stop you. Predominantly one for the girls, these sandals should ideally be worn with slightly cropped mom jeans (see page 16), in order to get a better cankle effect, and unpolished toenails. Boys, it's a fine line not to look like a pre-swim Michael Phelps, so lay off the sportswear anywhere else; consider adding a pair of white socks, and keep it casual with some knee-length jorts (see page 20).

TURTLENECK SWEATER

THE ESSENTIAL ITEM OF CLOTHING TO GUARANTEE YOU NEVER GET LAID

There must be some concern that if Normcore becomes truly pandemic, then there are going to be some serious problems with the birth rate. Maybe the fashion powers that be have been secretly in cahoots with climate-change bigwigs for years and have come up with this whole thing just to have fewer people on the planet. Screw the smallpox epidemic, dressing a whole generation in clothes that shriek celibacy and sexual unattractiveness will work wonders at getting the numbers down. And with no item is this more applicable than the turtleneck.

The beauty of a turtleneck is that it manages to be equally unattractive on both sexes. On men, it makes you look like you've got something to hide... a bestial amount of back hair? A tennis-ball-sized Adam's apple? An inclusion on a sex offender's register? And then there's what we'll call the foreskin factor: that little extra bit of material creeping up your neck, shrouding the lower half of your face... It's crying out for its own bris.

Over to the girls, and far from having something to hide, the unflattering shape of the turtleneck offers no place of sanctuary for anything resembling a female form. Large breasts? Your bosom will suddenly appear as if it stretches from waist to neck. Flat-chested? You'll succumb to foreskin face. Hourglass figure? It'll add ten pounds. Sold on it yet? If you need any more persuasion, remember you can only wear it black, which, aside from making you look like a jobbing puppeteer, will also suck the color and life from your complexion, rendering your skin tone firmly in the shade range usually reserved for Victorian consumptives.

For those concerned that all this still sounds far too attractive and that the prospect of sex is not yet extinguished fully, remember that you'll be tucking your turtle into the front wedgie of your stonewashed mom/dad jeans. Does a more effective method of contraception even exist?

FLEECE

N o, that header isn't a grammatical error: when it comes to Normcore, fleece is a way of life, not any one definable piece of clothing. That is why "the Fleece" would be a woefully inadequate way of describing this mandatory fabric.

Think not of your early 1990s fleeces. These were very much "The Fleece"—always in jacket form, often with a double zipper, and only available in colors the shade of elderly flesh (usually mottled beige). Those jackets simply won't cut it. Nor will the "Rave Fleece," which was sold exclusively at festivals, was covered with a psychedelic pattern, and whose sole purpose was to conceal the various and extensive body fluids that gathered upon your person over the course of the weekend. Saddest of all is that the "Animal Fleece" also hasn't been revived by Normcore. Sorry, wild packs of wolves running free over your wearer's gut, or proud stallions galloping across acres of back fat, you're still consigned to the QVC graveyard shift for now.

Now that you've cast aside your notions of traditional fleece, what the hell is a Normcore version? Well, basically the same as above but black and a bit more fitted. This rule actually can be applied to pretty much all Normcore fashion: keep it dark, make it for skinnier people, oh, and it doesn't have to be a jacket, either. Accessories such as gloves (for riding your third-hand mom bike—never a racy carbon-frame ride here, though a fold-up bike that pisses off everyone else on your train or bus is OK) or beanies (must be worn with caution and placed firmly on the head to avoid that hipster "I have an invisible sweet potato concealed under this" effect) are also firmly ensconced in Normcore fleece acceptability.

MULTIPACKS

I t's not strictly an item of clothing, but the concept of multiple-pack purchasing is a cornerstone of Normcore style and, as such, needs to be understood fully. When your aim is to look this similar to both yourself and everybody else daily, then multi-packing is the way to go. Treat the purchase of new clothes the same way you would toilet paper; you'd never buy just one, right (and if you do, we're never coming over)? So, what's acceptable to buy in bulk?

• THE WHITE TEE

Hit up Costco for packs of tees so cheap you could pretend you're Kanye West and throw them out after one wear. (N.B. You may also purchase black T-shirts in this fashion and, in extreme situations, for example if black and white examples are all sold out, gray will tide you over until the next delivery.)

• THE PLAID SHIRT

The halfway house between T-shirt and fleece, the plaid shirt is both perfectly unisex and also sexless. However, you have to wear it, never ever tie it around your waist.

• THE TUBE SOCKS

Wear anonymous brands if you can find them, but if you must go for a logo, a very small Nike swoosh may be permitted. To be worn pulled up to mid-calf, in the fashion of anti-DVT socks, with a choice of Jesus sandal or tennis shoe.

THE MOM JEAN

DIPPING INTO THE CLOSET OF YOUR GRANDMOTHER CAN UNCOVER SOME HIDDEN VINTAGE GEMS. SHAME THE SAME CAN'T BE SAID FOR THE 90'S MOTHER

Sick to death of searching for the perfect pair of jeans? That elusive pair that'll make your legs look longer, your butt higher, and your stomach flatter? Well, thank the Normcore gods for dispensing with such foolish notions of looking attractive in your clothes, and embrace the mom jean, where unflattering rules.

Not sure how to identify a mom jean? The first thing to watch out for is an absurdly long zip. We're talking about a fastening that even Dirk Diggler could make an entirely unhindered escape from. Next, draw your eyes up to the waistband. Constructed entirely of stretch elastic, this key design element has dual benefits. Firstly, the angry red welts across your, well, we'd stay stomach but some examples are so high it's more likely to be your lower chest, will remain for hours after you've kicked the jeans off, thus reminding you that even once disrobed you are suitably on trend. Secondly, it works in perfect harmony with the aforementioned long zip, adding yet another layer of unattractiveness in creating the perfect breeding ground for an admirable example of camel toe. Yep, the higher the pull into your unfortunate crotch, the far more fashionable you'll feel. Take note, in this instance the definition of "fashionable" can be interchanged with "symptoms of yeast infection."

At this point you may be a little worried that these denims, ugly as they are, still need that extra little push to make a proper statement to your fellow Normcore acolytes. This is the moment when you can easily add a few optional levels of anti-style. Shade is key; anything indigo is automatically off limits— it is far too flattering and aesthetically pleasing. Instead, stonewash is definitely your best bet; be sure to try a suits-no-skin gray for maximum effectiveness. An added bonus that comes with this color choice is that stonewash denim matches perfectly the ugly gray footwear that makes up another essential element of the Normcore uniform.

Extremes of tapering can add plenty of extra Normcore "kapow" to your jeans. Those in the know will always look to the vegetable patch for tailoring inspiration. Imagine the dimensions of a turnip with your thighs being the top and you're pretty much there— tourniquet-tight at the ankles, forming a lovely contrast to the windsock proportions from the hip to the knee.

THE BOMBER JACKET

NEVER BEFORE HAS A JACKET BEEN ADOPTED BY TWO SUCH DISPARATE GROUPS OF SOCIETY

Plucked straight from the gorilla-esque back of every provincial nightclub bouncer who's ever refused you entry owing to his obsession with filling a room with only non-sports-related footwear, the black nylon bomber is now a pillar of all Normcore wardrobes. Like its style sibling the fleece (see page 14), the bomber jacket enjoys the benefits of an elasticated waist and utilitarian zipper (buttons are largely uninvited to the Normcore party), but is far more of an evening option. This acknowledged, do not be tempted to lose your mind and indulge in such nonsense as a colored lining (the orange innards of the original MA-1 flight jackets need not apply), overly elastic cuffs, any kind of emblem, badge, typographic detailing, or the truly unthinkable—fur trim.

What's the easiest way to ensure you're getting your bomber purchase right? Ask yourself this: does it look expensive? If the answer is anything other than "I've eaten burgers that probably cost more," put it back on the shelf. You're aiming for a jacket that has the kind of vibe that suggests, "I got this free as a promotional item." And always remember that the thinner and less substantial the jacket, the better. Do not be foolish enough to think of this piece of clothing as offering you any kind of warmth or protection from the elements; that's not what it's there for. The true purpose of the jacket is the far more important one of signifying to everyone that your physical comfort comes a very low second to your style. Having said that, a bomber's clammy cheapness and synthetic materials might make you work up a bit of a sweat, so, you know, that's kind of keeping you cozy.

Addendum: For the extremely dedicated Norma or Norman, added style points can be gained, for both sexes, by buying the bomber jacket a size too small—thus rendering it even more useless as a functional item of clothing.

THE JORT

UNTIL SOMEONE INVENTS THE FLORT (OR FLEECE SHORT), THIS IS THE FIRST
ITEM IN THE SUITCASE FOR NORMCORERS ON A SUMMER VACATION

Fashion loves nothing more than a crappy portmanteau—the coatigan, the burqini, jeggings, greige... The list and the gradient of nonsensicalness is endless. Of course, not wanting to be left out, Normcore has its own version—meet the jort, a snazzy fusion of jeans and shorts, because clearly saying denim shorts takes up way too much time. Those valuable milliseconds wasted on that added enunciation could be far better spent sorting out your TiVo schedule for the week.

The jort is actually a very important item in both the male and female Normcorer's wardrobe, for it is only one of three pieces (the others being the unintentionally freezing bomber jacket and the bunion-breathable slider) that makes any concession to the fact that temperatures can sometimes rise above those experienced on a crisp winter morning. Try riding out a heat wave in cargo pants and garments made only from fleece or flannel fabrics. Without jorts, only the committed (and cold-blooded) Normcore aficionado could embrace this trend in anything but deepest winter.

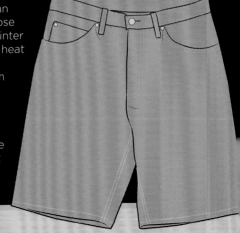

OF COURSE, THE DETAILING DIFFERS SLIGHTLY BETWEEN THE SEXES. THE MALE VERSUS FEMALE JORT BATTLE LINES ARE DRAWN AS FOLLOWS:

- **THE CUT**

  Female: High-waisted.
  Male: Normal-waisted.

- **THE FOOTWEAR**

  Female: Worn with no socks and sandals that wouldn't look out of place in a catalog of corrective footwear.
  Male: Socks may be worn, just ensure they are non-branded, sporty, white, and pulled up to mid-calf.

- **THE WASH**

  Female: You may experiment with differing tones—from deepest black through acid-wash gray.
  Male: Black or mid-blue—that's it boys, don't be getting fancy!

- **THE ACCOMPANIMENT**

  Female: The subtle crop top is the natural bedfellow of anything high-waisted, and, in a world where a hint of cleavage would be seen as criminally try-hard, it's a Normcore-approved way of flashing a little flesh.
  Male: Tucked in T-shirts with no logo, preferably bought in a multipack (see page 15); definitely no tank tops.

- **JORT NO-NOS FOR BOTH SEXES:**

  Hot pants, fraying, visible pockets, ribbed waistbands, any kind of embellishment, rips, and other nonsense.

THE TOURIST TRAP

IT'S ESSENTIAL TO LOOK LIKE A PASSENGER ON A COACH TRIP AT ALL TIMES, EVEN WHEN YOU'VE ONLY LEFT YOUR HOUSE TO PICK UP SOME MILK

Along with "Would my dad wear this?" one of the most useful questions you can ask yourself when trying to find your Normcore feet is: "Could I pass for a middle-aged, overweight tourist? Would someone try to steal my camera if I was traveling on the subway or underground system? Would anyone question me taking photographs of the out-of-work actors who have painted themselves gold and expect to be paid to sit in the same position all day? Will cab drivers turn a two-mile trip into a distance that, if I were to run it, would be considered an ultra marathon?" If the answer to all of the above is yes, then congrats. You've nailed it. Still floundering? Pick up a few of these key tourist items and fake it till you make it.

• THE LOCATION BASEBALL CAP

Emblazoned with something significant from your location—a sports team, the name of the capital city, a representation of a mundane provincial tourist attraction—but make sure it's not from anywhere too glamorous, so no Monaco/Maldives/Hawai'i, please. Think more of places national tax conferences might be held (and if the hat looks like it might have been given away free at one of these aforementioned conferences, even better).

• THE SECURE METHOD OF PERSONAL STORAGE

There's no better way to guarantee being pickpocketed than to take great lengths NOT to be pickpocketed—so for that authentic tourist vibe, invest in some super-secure ways to carry your stuff. The easiest thing to do is simply transfer your backpack into a front pack, creating a kind of luggage pregnancy bump and instantly marking you out as a stranger in the big city anxious about crime rates/finger-on-the-pulse Normcore trendsetter.

• THE LIGHTWEIGHT WINDBREAKER

There's only one criterion for this—it must be able to be rolled up into its own little bag and easily slotted into your back-to-front backpack. Almost entirely useless in rain heavier than a baby's dribble or wind stronger than a hotel-room hair dryer, it's a strange fusion of neither form nor functionality.

• THE LOGO TEE

Okay, you've had it drilled into you that a logo tee is about as welcome as Alexa Chung at a Weight Watchers meeting, but there is one style for which you can deviate from your plain black basic tee: the tourist logo tee. Follow the same rules as for the cap in terms of glamorous locales and avoid anything from the annoying twin franchises of "I heart" and "Keep Calm." Also keep an eye on the fit; on no account must it be tight-fitting, nor should you go down the path of "amusingly" retro. If a 48-year-old man with a 48-inch chest wouldn't wear it, then neither should you.

THE FANNY PACK VS THE BACKPACK

Because you can't always fit everything you need into the pockets of your cargo pants, what are Normcorers to do with all their stuff? "It" bags have been a no-no for years for everyone bar wealthy English aristos with triple-barreled titles; a clutch is far too Elizabeth Hurley; and those enormous totes the Olsen twins carry to make themselves look even more Borrowers-like are a definite no go.

So you have two choices: backpack or fanny pack. Neither has yet emerged as the carrier of choice, and with each having its own pros and cons, it's a battle likely to be waged for a while. (Still unsure? There's always secret option three—the concealed money belt. Staying true to the tourist as icon, it's a good bet for the next big thing.)

THE BACKPACK

CONS:

• The seemingly obvious Normcore brand of choice, Herschel, has already been claimed by those damn hipsters, seen on the backs of way too many cyclists half-standing on the pedals of their ironically retro bikes.

• You need to carry quite a bit of stuff to stop it from looking flaccid, and now that you've stopped going to the gym (see page 42 for a guide to your new Normcore body) and no longer have the need to tote around a sackful of sweaty clothes, your empty backpack will run the risk of looking like a recently discharged scrotal sack.

• The sweat factor—once you've piled on your wife-beater vest, your multipack tee, your plaid shirt, your cable-knit sweater vest, and your North Face down jacket, carrying a nylon sack on your back could tip you over the edge temperature-wise.

PROS:

• It gives you more personal space on public transport. Shove your back into the person behind you, and you've afforded yourself, and your bottom, at least two inches of extra room.

THE FANNY PACK

CONS:

• If you're wearing it over mom or dad jeans, it'll obscure your camel toe/moose knuckle, thus negating an important part of your Normcore look.

• You can't actually fit anything in it.

• The rave connotations— the question could be posed whether the fanny pack is too synonymous with rave culture ever truly to be accepted into the world of Normcore.

PROS:

• It's pretty secure—it's highly unlikely that you'd fail to notice anyone delving into your upper groin area, desperate to get his or her hands on your new Uniqlo loyalty card.

• Feeling too attractive in your outfit? A little too streamlined? And maybe even sexually attractive? Don't panic, a fanny pack is the purdah of purses, screening any hint of a desirable figure.

CHAPTER TWO:
ACHIEVING THE LOOK

THE BRANDS

A QUICK GUIDE TO WHO'S HOT AND WHO'S NOT IN THE
FASHION WORLD. YOU WANT THE LATTER

S o you know what to shop for
now, but where the hell to get
it? You might think you
can pick up your black tee,
ill-fitting knitwear, or made-
for-the-outdoors garments
anywhere, but you'd be
wrong. Very, very wrong
indeed...

• GAP

Nervous Normcorers out there, this store should be your first port of call. You won't need to seek out the nuances of the trend or be worried that a misjudged pocket on a shirt or a slightly too outré fabric will mark you out as a novice, because you could strip naked, blindfold yourself, douse your body in superglue, then ricochet off the rails, and still be winning. Basically everything in the whole shop, worn in any combination, will do. Gap is so confident of its premier Normcore status that it has even created its own name for it. Okay, it hasn't strayed a million miles with the #dressnormal tagline, but cheers for making it easy, guys.

TOP BUY: Chinos, the cut of which is tight on the crotch (regardless of the sex of your junk straining underneath it), baggy on the ass, and close to the thighs.

• NEW BALANCE

Having languished in the dad-trainer zone for decades, the sneakers that would have made you scream at your mom if she had bought them for you instead of Nikes are suddenly having their moment in the sun. A true bastion of Normcore, think of a pair of NBs like a Freemason's handshake: if you spot a pair, you've probably identified a like-minded Normcorer. Key to their success is their no-logo logo, so pick the black-on-black or gray-on-gray versions and leave maverick color combos like gray on black or black on gray to the unfashionable.

TOP BUY: The classic 574 has just the right amount of retro dad-ness.

• PATAGONIA

As one of the most environmentally conscious clothing producers out there, you might think it's a little too Eco-hipster, but you'd be incorrect. Because even if the closest you get to the outdoors is the smoking area outside your non-chain local bar (yep, Normcore might be a tough mistress when it comes to a lot of things, but she lets you do a heap of stuff that's bad for you), this all-weather, all-terrain brand is a master at rendering its wearer both sexless and shapeless.

TOP BUY: A paneled down jacket—basically a fat-suit masquerading as an item of clothing. It'll be a killer combo with your cargo pants.

• COS

Seeking a little mid-market blandness? No one does it like the Euro high street. Cos is queen, but any store that sells more black clothing—over 60 percent—than other colors of womenswear works, too, (see also Zara and Maje). Still, added points must go to Cos for its experiments with structure. It understands the Normcore/Amish correlation when it comes to flaunting your body, so a well-placed concertina fold here, girth-giving pleat there, or amputee-effect sleeve all add up to a no-brainer Normcore look.

TOP BUY: A black dress that, in an emergency, could easily double as a windsock.

BIRKENSTOCK

Because you can't wear sneakers every day of your life, when your NBs need an airing, turn to the orthopedic sandal favored by dinner ladies, nurses, and bunion sufferers everywhere. An example of the you-need-to-be-beautiful-to-get-away-with-being-this-ugly school of Normcore, if you're not tanned, toned, and immaculately dressed from head to toe, then topping off your look with anything from this German brand (yes, even the mega-cozy fur-lined ones) will end in disaster. The problem mainly lies in the foot-widening properties; on anything less than a perfectly pedicured paw, the unfortunate transformation from normal feet to a pair of past-their-best sea bass is instantaneous.

TOP BUY: Well, a pair of Birkenstocks would be a good starting point.

bender diary entry from Lindsay Lohan. And with a plain jersey tank from their 2014 fall/winter collection coming in at a whopping $235 (and no, the purchase doesn't come with a gift of two $100 bills), this is not really very normal at all.

TOP BUY: The same-price-as-a-mini-break T-shirts, of course.

• FRUIT OF THE LOOM

If you thought it had died a quiet death, found only as neglected, faded reincarnations in dusty forgotten wardrobes at your parents' house, and only brought out on home-improvement days, you'd be right. Until the precise moment

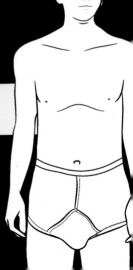

IS IT NORM OR NOT?

By now you should be aware of what items of clothing to look out for, and also which brands to covet. But sometimes buying an outfit that's suitably bland and uninspiring ain't as simple as it seems. Luckily, here is a list of simple questions you can ask yourself to determine whether the piece of clothing you are considering is sufficiently Normcore:

1. WHEN I WAS A KID, WOULD I BE BULLIED AT SCHOOL FOR WEARING THIS?
YES: It's Norm
NO: It's Not

2. DOES THE STORE I AM IN ALSO SELL CAMPING EQUIPMENT AND OUTDOOR SPORTING GOODS?
YES: It's Norm
NO: It's Not

3. DID MY MOM/DAD WEAR ONE OF THESE WHEN (S)HE TOOK ME TO SEE JURASSIC PARK FOR MY BIRTHDAY ONE YEAR?
YES: It's Norm
NO: It's Not

4. IF I BUY THIS, WILL IT DECREASE MY CHANCES OF GETTING LAID?
YES: It's Norm
NO: It's Not

5. DID I SEE CHANDLER WEARING SOMETHING VERY SIMILAR IN THE ONE WHERE ROSS AND RACHEL TAKE A BREAK?
YES: It's Norm
NO: It's Not

6. IS IT BLACK, WHITE, GRAY, BROWN, OR SLUDGE GREEN?
YES: It's Norm
NO: It's Not

CHAPTER THREE:

NORMCORE ICONS

SEINFELD

Now that you're some way through this book and have more than a working knowledge of what it takes to be Normcore, you may find yourself with some questions about this new lifestyle you're about to adopt. And surely the first one is, "What about smart-casual dress codes?"

Yep, zip-up fleeces, overly pocketed cargo pants, and multipack Gap T-shirts might be fine for walking your consciously un-bred dog or on an eight-hour Netflix binge, but what about a fancy brunch? A dress-down Friday in a formal office? The weeknight engagement party of someone who's more of an acquaintance than a friend? What does a true Normcorer don for such tricky in-between situations? He simply thinks WWSD—What would Seinfeld do?

If you're not au fait with the nuances of the comedy character's wardrobe, then simply think of it thus: it's the

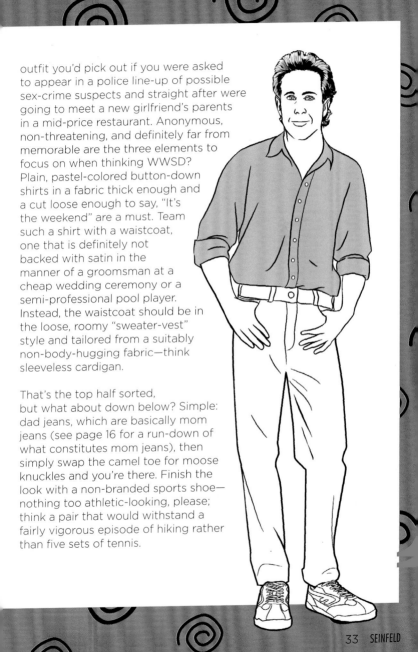

outfit you'd pick out if you were asked to appear in a police line-up of possible sex-crime suspects and straight after were going to meet a new girlfriend's parents in a mid-price restaurant. Anonymous, non-threatening, and definitely far from memorable are the three elements to focus on when thinking WWSD? Plain, pastel-colored button-down shirts in a fabric thick enough and a cut loose enough to say, "It's the weekend" are a must. Team such a shirt with a waistcoat, one that is definitely not backed with satin in the manner of a groomsman at a cheap wedding ceremony or a semi-professional pool player. Instead, the waistcoat should be in the loose, roomy "sweater-vest" style and tailored from a suitably non-body-hugging fabric—think sleeveless cardigan.

That's the top half sorted, but what about down below? Simple: dad jeans, which are basically mom jeans (see page 16 for a run-down of what constitutes mom jeans), then simply swap the camel toe for moose knuckles and you're there. Finish the look with a non-branded sports shoe— nothing too athletic-looking, please; think a pair that would withstand a fairly vigorous episode of hiking rather than five sets of tennis.

ROSEANNE CONNER

A TRUE STORY: THE CACKLE OF ROSEANNE DURING THE OPENING CREDITS OF HER EPONYMOUS SHOW WAS CAUSED BY THE HILARITY OF THE SUGGESTION THAT ONE DAY SHE'D BE CONSIDERED A FASHION ICON

Female Normcore icons are few and far between. With unisex being very much the rule of thumb, it's largely the boys who have emerged as inspiration. However, if we delve back a decade or so, there's one lady who had this whole thing sorted even then: the mighty Roseanne Conner. Played by Roseanne Barr, this eponymous heroine was winning at all aspects of Normcore lifestyle from 1988 to 1997 and thus is possibly the earliest recorded example of the style discipline. From her plaid shirts and home-permed hair to her sofa slobbing and series of "couldn't-give-one" jobs, she was doing it before today's trend forecasters were even a twinkle in the lens of their daddy's thick-rimmed glasses.

How can we convert this look for the modern woman about town, though? Here are a few key Roseanne-specific items to snap up.

- **THE CLIP-IN HAIR BOW**
  This seems to go against the laws of unnecessary adornment (it's like iconoclasm for Normcore), but it's just ugly enough to work. Where the hipsters claimed the scrunchie, the frumpy bow will belong to Normcore.

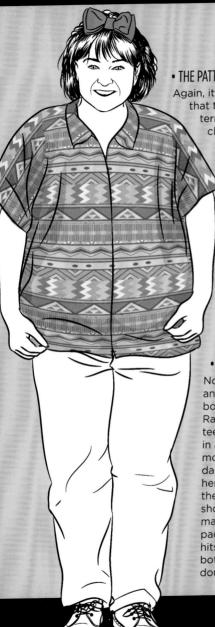

• THE PATTERNED SHIRT

Again, it's the unattractiveness that tips this into Normcore territory: the colors need to clash and the print itself should in no way be pleasing to the eye—think oversize sofa-print florals, retina-jarring Aztec shapes, or anything you'd see painted on the side of a bumper car at the fairground. If colors cover just the top third of the shirt, western style, that's fine, but watch out for the fit—one size fits all up to an XXXL is your safest bet.

• THE GRANDDAD BLAZER

Not to be confused in any way with the cutesy boyfriend blazers worn by Rachel Zoe-bots to look teeny-weeny, as if drowning in a big boy's jacket. This is more country-club dinner dance. Boxy is the key word here; your waist should look the same width as your shoulders (which may or may not have a little padding), and make sure it hits the exact point of your bottom to make it look double its size.

STEVE JOBS

Y ou've been introduced to the concept of mom jeans, but whereas poor old mater only gets a bit of denim, pops gets a whole sub-genre, and for the finest example of dad-dressing we look to the unsurpassed daddy of all things Normcore, the late, great Steve Jobs.

The tech titan had all the cash in the world, but still chose to wear pretty much the same thing every day—a uniform of non-(visibly) branded dad clothes: a black turtleneck (and yes, he was a victim of foreskin face), ill-fitting Levi's 501 jeans, and white sneakers. This is how to do inconspicuous Normcore: pick a uniform and stick to it. Admittedly, the turtlenecks were Issey Miyake, custom-made for him by the designer, and he had at least a hundred of them.

Further evidence for Jobs's Normdaddy status is the fact that he tried to get all of Apple to wear the same thing—a nylon jacket designed by Miyake. His staff booed him off the stage—little did they know they were on the cusp of a style revolution, and one of those nylon windbreakers would probably buy half a dozen new iPhones today.

LIZ LEMON

Like Roseanne Conner before her, we have to look to the world of comedy for our next female icon (could this constant symmetry with the world of making people laugh have anything... ANYTHING to tell us about this trend? What could it possibly be saying...?). And we land firmly upon the unfortunate Liz Lemon, Tina Fey's character in *30 Rock*. Now, Fey herself is almost, almost on the border of being a Normcore Icon, but sadly her bangs are often a little too sassy, and her necklines are often not androgynous enough to confuse the world about her sex, so that puts her out of the running. Liz, on the other hand, is in enough denial about dressing as a sexually attractive adult female to be an effective example.

Prescription glasses bought purely for their functionality are the jump-off for her qualification in Normcore-Icon proficiency. Not heavily rimmed enough to be hipster, nor slim enough to be face-framing, they must take some responsibility for the lack of sex in her life, although she has a totally Normcore attitude to this, too, preferring coitus to be fast, non-existent, or "only on Saturdays."

Liz Loves...

• LESBIAN FOOTWEAR (it's a thing, really!): Her choice of shoes leads a friend to assume she's gay—a Normcore-style triumph.

• GENDER-NEUTRAL CLOTHES: If the charity shop didn't know which section to put it in, it's a sure way to say that it came from Liz's wardrobe.

• SLANKETS: That's a blanket with sleeves, for the uninitiated (and uncomfortable).

KATE AND WILLS

THE DUKE AND DUCHESS OF CAMBRIDGE HAVE BEEN IDENTIFIED BY THE MEDIA AS THE COUPLE WHO WILL PROVIDE THE BRITISH MONARCHY WITH A MUCH-NEEDED INJECTION OF COOL. GOD HELP US ALL

Post-hipsters seeking style refuge, you ain't gonna like this. The premier example of coupled-up Normcore is to be found in the heart of the British royal family. Yep, Kate and Wills are, without equal, definitely the duke and duchess (and eventual king and queen) of Normcore.

Vogue UK first called Kate out as the Duchess of Normcore—and we don't think they meant it as a compliment, the catty things—while an off-duty Wills possibly holds the record for most Normcore staples worn at any one time. It's quite the phenomenon, the posh (especially the British posh) being at the forefront of fashion. Where else would you find a woman whose main concern is to look like her mother, and a man whose main concern is to find a woman to sleep with who looks like his mother?

Quell some of the panic you feel in your quasi-hipster souls that a man who chooses to wear a pinky ring and a woman in American tan five-deniers are more on trend than you. Instead, let's re-categorize them as Poshnorm and turn to them as inspiration for those occasions where it's tricky to turn up as if en route to a mild-peril adventure holiday or being forced to attend a work-organized, team-building activity day. Girls, ditch Kate's blow out, but embrace her natural-toned hair and the fact that she occasionally allows a few grays to peek through—the slovenly wench. Her trademark nude wedges are yours for the taking, along with her collection of mall-bought sneakers and Breton jumpers, and her habit of top-to-toe dressing in just one color.

Gents, William's tourist manner of dress (ironic to look like a tourist when he kind of owns the United Kingdom, so is effectively always at home) is Normcore 101 from the top of his novelty baseball cap to the bottom of his sturdy walking boots. He is the perfect example of unsurpassed inoffensiveness.

DAWSON LEERY

Actually, let's make that EVERYONE from *Dawson's Creek* (well, apart from Jen, who showed far too much eye-catching cleavage to really qualify; nice try with the home perm and the bank-clerk uniform slacks, but those extra undone buttons on your pinstripe smart/casual shirts instantly put you out of the running!), because, in fact, it's the very interchangeability of their wardrobes that really marks the cast out as the founding pilgrims of the Normcore movement. Would you really have noticed if Pacey accidentally donned one of Dawson's sweater vests? If Joey poached one of Jack's cable knits? We think not. No wonder it took so goddamned long for any of them to get it on with one another. They couldn't be quite sure whose teen abs were going to be hiding underneath those communal button-downs.

A closer look at the cast's beauty and grooming habits reveals them to be even more ahead of the Normcore game than we first assumed. From the girls, we have Jen's aforementioned DIY curls, Joey's sweeping curtain of hair, as untouched as her plain white cotton-brief-encased lady parts, and Andie's shampoo-shy, mousier-than-an-abandoned-church bob, each one just waiting for you to take it to the salon to complete your head-to-toe Normcore makeover.

Over to the boys, and everything goes a little bit barbershop window posters, circa 1992. Choose from brushed-forward demi-bangs, not weighed down by any styling product, à la Pacey Witter, or a pre-military-entrance regulation chop like Jack's. For those chaps possibly suffering a teeny tiny bit from a prematurely receding hairline, or someone keen to disguise a fivehead, Dawson's let-it-all-hang-out parted curtains, kept in place solely by RSI-inducing hand-sweeping movements, is the cut of choice.

BARACK OBAMA

H e's a man of firsts, and he's gone and done it again... Meet America's first Normcore President. Possibly the best example of the dressing-as-a-tourist ethos so key to the heart of Normcore, from double denim (aka the Canadian tuxedo) for a phone call to Putin, to his middle-manager-of-a-small-bank blue button-downs, he's got that out-of-town dad look to a tee. He's even been spotted in Norm Mecca, Gap, buying only crew necks for his family, wary of the dangers of a V-neck tee—something about them slipping, apparently. Well, thank God he avoided that pitfall and America can sleep soundly knowing that neither the President nor the First Lady will have any precarious neckline indiscretions. Phew.

Other indicators elevating Obama to presidential Norm status include his sunglasses that have just enough lack of style surely to be prescriptive, his golf wardrobe (sometimes worn off the green, too), and the fact that his security men have better-cut suits than he. All even more impressive when you consider the lack of support he receives in these endeavors from his wife, Michelle, who constantly falls prey to some common novice Normcore pitfalls. Here's where she's going wrong:

- Lanvin sneakers—the thought is there, wearing workout shoes with everyday wear, but buy something less attractive for God's sake, woman.

- Embellished necklines—why ruin a perfectly unremarkable sweater with attention-seeking detail? For future reference, when in doubt about acceptable levels of self-decoration, just say WWTAD—what would the Amish do?

- J. Crew—you're too late, love. Should've got in there when they used the *Dawson's Creek* cast as models back in '98, there were no baroque cocktail pants then.

- Yoga pants—again, you're making the sportswear mistake. We can see you're trying, but abandon these figure-hugging, butt-enhancing flights of fancy for a pair of your husband's faded joggers, please.

CHAPTER FOUR:

NORMCORE LIFESTYLE

NORM BODY

FORGET THE 5:2 DIET, OR EATING ONLY THE SAME FOOD AS A DISGRUNTLED PICTISH CHIEFTAIN, VEGAN CAVEMAN, OR LACTOSE-INTOLERANT T-REX, A MAJOR BENEFIT OF THE NORMCORE LIFE IS THAT YOU CAN EAT WHAT YOU LIKE

Still not really ready to commit to the Normcore lifestyle? Maybe you're a little concerned about giving up your hipster luxuries in return for a wardrobe that borders on Amish. Well, Normcore has a little trick up its sleeve to sweeten (literally) the deal.

Say hello to the Normcore body and goodbye to your no-wheat/gluten/dairy/flavor past, regain feeling in your previously numb-from-spinning nether regions, and return to a world where trainers don't mean training. The Normcore body works on the principle that Normcore fashion staples already look like they add ten pounds, so no one is going to notice if you really are packing a little extra. And, best of all, there's something to disguise every flaw.

BIG BUTT

The plaid shirt is your NBF (new butt friend). Illegal to wear tucked in, it'll cover up years of squat skipping. Serious problem on your hands? In extreme circumstances we'll allow you to tie it round your waist for a little 90s grunge twist on your descent into morbid obesity.

GENEROUS THIGHS

The mom jean was made for you. If you don't have a generous circumference (think Cara Delevingne's waist), then these create just that, thus eliminating any point in striving for a thigh gap. As an extra plus point, the depth to which these sink into the crotch also means the chafing that your new larger limbs could cause is happily eliminated.

MUFFIN TOP

Got a little overspill even with the lack of forgiving mom/dad denims? Don't panic, simply reach for a vest. With the figure-forgiving characteristics of a tabard, it creates a boxy outline of even the slimmest mid-section and becomes the fall guy for your lack of a waist.

NORMCORE EXERCISE

A BLAND LIFESTYLE SHOULD ENCOURAGE AN INTEREST IN BORING SPORTS. YES, WE'RE LOOKING AT YOU CHESS TOURNAMENTS, FIVE-DAY CRICKET MATCHES, THREE-WEEK CYCLE RACES, AND LONG-DISTANCE RUNNING

Okay, so we've told you that on your journey to becoming fully Normcore, you can ditch the 5am SoulCycle class and reintroduce foodstuffs other than kale and quinoa into your everyday diet. But with the fashion movement already foretelling some population issues (to recap: lack of sexiness equates with lack of sex, and with artificial insemination not yet being mainstream, we're going to see a dip in the birth rate), we can't afford the existing population to fast forward to their deaths because exercise has become unnecessary.

So you no longer have to show off professional athlete-standard pecs in deep V-tees or Victoria's Secret model glutes in Hervé Leger body con. But if diabetes or only being able to leave the house when a television show stages an intervention and breaks down your bedroom wall and carries you out with a forklift doesn't sound all that desirable (plus New Balance don't do a wide fit), what's a Normcorer to do to keep within the confines of a non-fatal BMI?

HIKING

Actually, let's call this out for what it is. Walking. Yep, it's okay to walk; sometimes when a train or moving walkway isn't at hand, you may have to put one foot in front of the other, and with the classic hiking footwear (kind of a sturdier hi-top in shades of sludge) being Normcore standard issue, you've already got the kit.

CYCLING

For anyone who has known cycling only within a hipster framework, it may come as a surprise to know that not only does it sometimes happen outside, on a bike that's not fixed to the ground, minus a Lycra-clad automaton shouting "encouragement," but also it can occur on bikes that cost less than your monthly rent and that don't have a specially designed aerodynamic folding frame/cupcake-specific basket. The Normcore cyclist chooses a second-hand rust bucket and uses it for the crazy concept of actually getting to places. Lunatic.

SPORTS YOU CAN DO WITH A DRINK IN YOUR HAND

Britain excels at this, so look to its shores for inspo. Darts, snooker, bingo (okay, so this last one isn't strictly exercise, but you can work up a sweat with your dabber), anything that might take place in a pub or bar is an acceptable sport. Note: the hipster fetishization of table tennis immediately disqualifies this from the above status.

NORMCORE SEXLIFE

FUNCTIONAL RATHER THAN FUN, AWKWARD RATHER THAN AWESOME, PASSIVE RATHER THAN PASSIONATE... IT'S THE NORMS WHO PUT THE COY IN COITUS

So when the basis of a trend is that it dials down the desire to be attractive—what the hell does that mean for the bedroom (and we mean bedroom; the shower/garden/car/bathroom of the local artisanal cupcake boutique would be far too extravagant for Normcore sex)? We've voiced our anxieties about what the total enshrinement of all erogenous zones could do for the planet, but as it doesn't look as though anyone is paying attention, here's how to do it Normcore-style.

DOS:
- Do keep it behind closed doors, on nice clean sheets.
- Do do it at a normal, sensible time, like Saturday night after a movie, or Sunday morning. Only crazy, sex-mad hipster types have time to stay up on a Tuesday or waste a whole Saturday being naked.
- Do think about retro contraception; the diaphragm with its simple, clean lines and shape suddenly feels very now. And if functionality, reliability, or efficacy isn't what you look for in a contraceptive, then the withdrawal method is having a moment.
- Do think about your mum and dad—yep, traditionally number-one option for boner killing, your parents' style of doing it should now be your framework for your own sex life.

DON'TS:

- Don't even think about whips, crops, or any kind of "erotic" S&M-like props. If there's one thing Normcore stands up against, it's the sodding Fifty Shades effect.
- Don't be too impromptu; consider scheduling in a regular weekly time slot.
- Don't expect to be able to have a quickie. Have you ever tried to rip open a flannel shirt? Ain't gonna happen.

Acceptable Positions

- MISSIONARY: It's a given.

- DOGGY: Because as the Bloodhound Gang said—you can both watch *The X-Files*.

- SIXTY-NINE: Now the men have shaved off their hipster beards, the whole thing is a lot more comfortable.

GROOMING

It's okay, we're not talking about that kind of grooming. There might be a lot to put you off this trend, but nothing that'll land you a 10–15-year prison sentence in the vulnerable prisoner wing. We promise. Instead, it is of course the etiquette of what the hell to do with your hair and beauty, because there's no point in reverse trending your whole wardrobe only to ruin it all with some way-too-jazzy highlights or a miscalculated goatee now, is there?

BOYS

• Beards: When even Justin Bieber has tried out artisan facial hair and the hipsters are so bored with beards that they've taken to stuffing theirs with flowers, the death knell for any kind of facial fuzz has well and truly sounded. So it's clean-shaven and anonymous all the way. Not too clean-shaven, mind you, but also not too unkempt. Sorry, it's not that easy: five o'clock shadow is okay, 80s "designer" stubble is not, so think George Clooney at the end of a shift as Dr. Doug Ross in *ER* rather than George Michael at the end of a... well, you can finish that sentence for yourself.

• Hair: All hail the end of the half-and-half, that ridiculous hairstyle consisting of what looks like a splayed guinea pig on the top, sometimes fashioned into a quiff, with shaved sides. A resurrection of a hairstyle last popular post-WW1, it's had men walking round resembling grown-out Brazilian bikini waxes for far too long. If it does nothing else, once Normcore inspires a backlash against this, it will have contributed greatly to society. But what replaces it? Anything that your hairdresser might describe as "neat," so imagine pre-job interview/ court appearance/army conscription and you're there.

GIRLS

"No makeup" makeup is utter nonsense that magazines try to peddle you, which somehow results in you needing to buy three times as many things as "regular makeup" makeup requires, but we're sad to say that's just what you're going to need to perfect the Normcore look. Ugly clothes need pretty faces, and when you can't be seen to be making any effort, it's your only option. Here's a starter guide:

• Face: Flawless skin is essential when your wardrobe drains every scrap of color from your face. If you're not keen on the open-casket cadaver complexion, you need a bare minimum of foundation, concealer, and blusher. All expertly blended so as to be invisible, obviously. As a genuinely useful tip—cream blush over BB cream is the easiest way to "I haven't bothered" prettiness.

• Eyes: Black is definitely not back, and false eyelashes are practically iconoclastic. All anyone who isn't blessed with Bambi lashes has to compensate is brown mascara—look, you're lucky it's not soot from the fire, so just get on with it.

• Lips: Far too sexual to draw attention to, you get Chapstick (and just regular at that, never the tinted or outrageously flavored options), and that's your lot.

• Perfume: 90s body sprays rule. Think Teen Spirit, Charlie, or Impulse. At a push, a little splash of CK One as it'll render you olfactorily sexless, or Anaïs Anaïs for the genuine mom.

NORM PUBES

To truly commit to the cause, external appearance isn't enough. Yes, you look the part, but the question is "How can I be Normcore when naked?" The answer lies in the politics of pubes. What you do with your topiary speaks volumes about your faith in the movement. For guys, it's simple: do nothing. For ladies, it's complicated. It's likely you've tried a full bush and the odd Brazilian, but Normcore vetoes both of these. A tricky master, it's not even okay to sport a high-leg bikini (aka the wax where you keep your undies on). Nope, Normcore demands a combo of all of the above... Yep, the Normwax leaves all your undercarriage (aka the super painful bits to wax) totally bare, with a retro full plume sitting above. This demands all the awkwardness of disrobing and lying with your legs at angles usually only seen during removal of accidentally inserted internal foreign objects in the ER, but none of the useful won't-look-like-I'm-keeping-spiders-in-my-swimsuit properties.

NORMCORE
PETS

THE CRUX OF THE NORMCORE MINDSET IS TO AVOID STANDING OUT AT ALL
COSTS. THE SAME RULE MUST BE APPLIED TO YOUR ANIMAL COMPANIONS

With over-bred canines and unattractive but rare cats having had their moment in the hipster sun, it's now the turn of mutts and moggies. French bulldogs, Boston terriers, and teacup Yorkies, your time is up. Creepily eared/ skinned/faced pussies—you, too. Cultivated mutts—Cockapoos, Labradoodles, Wotties (yep, they're a thing: Rottweiler and West Highland terriers... Google it if you don't believe us), and Poosatians (okay, not really a thing. Yet)—you're also out of the running. Pets of no discernible parentage rule.

Once you've chosen your mongrel, preferably from a rescue home (added points if they're minus a limb or eyeball), and brought him or her home, you first need to name them. Anything an A-lister might call their offspring is immediately off the list. Think, instead, as with so many facets of Normcore life, of dads. There's no better Normcore moniker for your new pet than one that you wouldn't be surprised to find also belonged to your buddy's dad—Steve, Kevin, Rodney, and Wayne would all work (a word of warning, do not be tempted to go back further into the names of granddads— your Alfreds, Winstons, and Arthurs are too hipster).

What if your rental agreement/commitment to cycling holidays/ hours at the insurance firm don't permit a cat or dog?

THE ALTERNATIVES:

• Small Furries

Rabbits are instantly discounted owing to their current fashion gentrification (thanks Cara Delevingne), but there are other options. Anything you might have had in your junior-high classroom is a good starting point, so hamster, gerbil, guinea pig— all fine. Anything quirkier than that—we're talking ferrets, chinchillas, and degus—is far too showy. Vermin are discounted, too. Would your mom willingly let rats or mice share your home? No she would not, and nor will the Normcore let you.

• Fish

Specifically the kind you might win at the fair—if they need specialist foods/aquariums/lights/personal hypnotherapists, they're out. On no account must you have a large, showy tank with miniature castles; it's a basic glass bowl only.

• Tortoise

The ultimate low-fi pet, you could easily forget you had one of these chaps for a year or so and he'd be perfectly fine. Probably. Don't try it though, eh?

NORMCORE TV

EXCITED ABOUT THE NEW SERIES OF BETTER CALL SAUL OR GOTHAM? DON'T BE, THEY'RE NOT FOR YOU. IF THE PRESS OR PEOPLE AT WORK ARE TALKING ABOUT IT, YOU SHOULDN'T BE WATCHING IT. STICK TO THE OLD STUFF

F or those of us who like our clothes to make us look better, not worse, Normcore may seem so far rather unappealing. But before you discount the movement as a way of life because of your stance on fleece, listen up: it's now okay to own a television and watch programs when they're actually on. You no longer have to pretend not to have watched shows on anything but your Mac for the last ten years. It doesn't matter that you don't know how to download illegally, have Netflix only because you couldn't work out how to cancel it after your free month's trial, and still buy physical box sets of DVDs—that's absolutely fine now. If all that sounds a little bit too easy and you're uncomfortable with the idea of a fashionable lifestyle that isn't actually making your life harder, don't worry, there are still a few rules to abide by.

SCANDI IS OKAY
Yep, subtitled dramas focused on Nordic jumpers or their US adaptations might have been picked over and discarded by the hipsters, but that makes them prime roadkill for any passing Normcorer to latch onto. You don't want to be first with

anything (this rule also applies to comedy—*Friends*, *Seinfeld*, and *Curb Your Enthusiasm* reruns on Comedy Central should be your cornerstones), and it can't be too obscure. As a rule of thumb, it should appear on basic cable, it shouldn't be less than a year old, and your mom should be able to recognize the title.

BINGE WATCHING IS KING

Doing nothing for an entire weekend but watching a box set that everyone else saw years ago is perfectly acceptable—try *The Wire*, *Breaking Bad*, and the first series of *Orange is the New Black* (however, you'll need to let the dust settle first before starting season two).

KEEP IT HOMELY

Baking, knitting, craft, gardening, antiques—shows based on classes offered by your local senior-citizens' center are classic Normcore fodder.

NORM HOME

Y ou'd think the Normcore home would be easy to identify, create, and maintain, but no, it has so many nuances and fine lines that one whisper of inappropriate blanket stitch on your locally bought cushions or a hint of reclamation about your coffee table and you're done. The safest option? Buy it all at Ikea. With flat-pack furniture assembly being a bona fide Normcore hobby, you're killing two birds with one stone.

Once assembled, do not be tempted to personalize with some cute "life hack" you saw on Buzzfeed to give your apartment a French cottage/shabby chic/Aztec kingdom feel. THESE ARE NOT THINGS. Not in Normcore land, anyway. Build it, then use it. Shop for it like you do wine in a restaurant, buy one up from the most basic and put up with it regardless of the outcome.

CHECKLIST:

- Blinds NOT curtains
- Hard-wearing carpet NOT sanded wooden floors
- Shower cubicle NOT wet room
- Microwave NOT Nutribullet
- Doorbell NOT Doorknocker
- Ikea prints NOT limited-edition work
- Breakfast bar NOT dining table
- Wallpaper NOT paint
- House phone NOT cell phone

If you manage to move in somewhere that the realtor describes as "in need of renovation," and the previous owner died there (of natural causes; murder scenes spoil the vibe somewhat—old age is your aim), then you've hit the jackpot. Snap it up, barter the price down for all the "work" you're going to have to do, then kick back in your avocado bathroom suite and congratulate yourself on being so terribly fashion forward.

NØRM HÜS

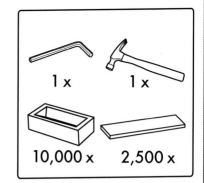

1 x   1 x

10,000 x   2,500 x

FLAT PACK

1.

2.

LIFE EVENTS

By now, you'll be pretty confident at being Normcore in most aspects of your daily life. You'd never buy a pair of flattering jeans or order a drink that comes in a jam jar, and you haven't watched any TV series from post-1999 for months. But there are still going to be occasions that throw you. One can't, for example, go to a wedding wearing fleece, nor can you celebrate the birth of a child with a box set, and just try heading to a funeral in a Canadian tuxedo. Don't worry, though—now you're this far into it, you're ready for events that call for "Advanced Norm." Here's how...

• WEDDING

Your usual arsenal of fabrics is going to be tricky to smuggle into formal nuptials. Aside from the heat factor—try busting out your signature "Oops Upside Your Head"-rowboat move in down and plaid—one glimpse of your outfit and the nearest bridesmaid/mother of the bride/busybody will have you at best ejected, at worst relegated to the aunts' table in seconds.

What to do? Fool them with illusion. Can anyone tell that those aren't in fact tuxedo pants but are, instead, just black elastic jeans? Did you buy your shirt in a multipack? Could you say that you're wearing hiking boots because of an orthopedic issue? Do all of the above and you can consider yourself in the very top Normcore percentile.

• BABIES

When it comes to how to deal with the miracle of new life, it's more a list of do nots.

Do not…
…announce the pregnancy via a sonogram on your social media. You shouldn't really be using anything other than Bebo, Yahoo messenger, and MySpace anyway, and last time we looked, they weren't too accommodating for that kind of thing. In a world where undoing a button could have you shunned by the style elite, we're guessing a photograph of one of your internal organs won't go down too well either.

…give your child a weird name. Weird in this case expands to encompass anything "ironically" retro, anything conception-location based, and anything with phonetically unnecessary letters—Zooey Deschanel, we're looking at you.

…spend more on baby outfits than you do on your own. Does your Normkid need baby Dior? Does he hell.

…become an organic-bore. Home-grown, home-made, home-regurgitated individual portions of sweet potato and kale slops? What's wrong with a jar of microwaved Heinz or Cow & Gate?

• FUNERALS

The trickiest of all—because even those at the very top echelons of style do need to show a little respect sometimes. But there are ways around it. Were you terribly close to the person in question? Easy, just sit smugly in your Uniqlo vest and denim shorts telling everyone he confided in you months ago that that's what he wanted everyone to wear to his funeral. It's not like he's going to call you out on it now, is it? Weren't that close? Trickier but still do-able. How about you invent a recent career change as an EMT and pretend that you're currently on call? No one's going to argue with your fleece and cargo combo then.

CHAPTER FIVE:

JUST HOW NORMCORE ARE YOU?

CONGRATULATIONS, YOU'VE READ THIS WHOLE GUIDE AND ARE NOW SO BLAND THAT SEVERAL PEOPLE HAVE PROBABLY ALREADY MISTAKEN YOU FOR A LAMP-POST THIS MORNING ALONE. BUT HAS IT ALL GONE IN? ONLY ONE WAY TO FIND OUT—IT'S TEST TIME!

Over the next five pages you will find 15 simple questions that have been painstakingly formulated by brightest minds from the most prestigious schools across the globe to determine where exactly you sit on the Normcore spectrum.

1. WHAT IS COS?

A: A snazzy abbreviation for "because" that you can use in cute texts to your boo along with your fave emoticons

B: A crunchy and refreshing lettuce variety

C: A Swedish fashion brand, offering architecturally designed style within a minimalistic framework

2. WHO OF THE FOLLOWING IS NOT A NORMCORE STYLE ICON?

A: Your dad
B: Jerry Seinfeld
C: The woman behind the register at your local gas station

3. PUBIC HAIR—WHERE DO YOU STAND?

A: Standard porn issue please—if I couldn't draw an anatomically correct image of the genitalia in question, I'm not interested
B: Holidays and high days and I might get the clippers out
C: A reverse mullet, long on top, short underneath

4. WHICH OF THE FOLLOWING I S THE CORRECT DEFINITION OF A CANADIAN TUXEDO?

A: A complicated sex position involving restraints around the neck and speaking in a funny accent
B: The outfit your cousin from Vancouver wore to your sister's wedding
C: A double-denim two piece, consisting of either jeans and denim shirt or jeans and jean jacket

5. WHAT IS THE ACCEPTABLE NUMBER OF POCKETS ON THE FRONT OF A CARGO PANT?

A: Two—I've only got two hands to shove in them, right?
B: Does it really matter?
C: Four—two at the waist, two mid-thigh

6. WHAT'S A SLIDER?

A: A fun thing to play on at the park
B: An inevitable descent into something undesirable
C: A super-cool unisex rubber sports shoe rediscovered as fashion nirvana

7. HOW MANY DEFINING CHARACTERISTICS OF MOM JEANS CAN YOU NAME?

A: Ummm, they're denim?
B: They're kind of unflattering?
C: Elastic waist, high cut, tapered leg, acid wash, baggy ass, you want me to go on...?

8. WHAT'S GAP'S NORMCORE STRAPLINE?

A: Bend and Snap
B: Couldn't give a fuck
C: Dress Normal

9. WHAT WOULD YOU DRINK ON A NIGHT OUT?

A: A cupcake-flavored Bellini, served in a jam jar topped with super-cute faux frosting
B: A gin and tonic
C: A bottle of Rolling Rock, no glass

10. WHICH OF THE FOLLOWING ISN'T A NORMCORE PORTMANTEAU?

A: A jort
B: Greige
C: A jackumper

11. WHAT'S YOUR FAVORITE COLOR?

A: Pink or purple or—hang on, what day is it today? Wednesday, well then it's probably sky blue
B: Don't really have one. I'm not 11
C: Why are you even asking this? Obviously it's black, or occasionally faded black

12. WHAT'S HANGING ON YOUR WALL?

A: Cute clip frames with all your gal pals drinking cocktails
B: A couple of pictures you took on vacation displayed in kind of plain-ish frames
C: Nothing

13. YOU GO TO THE GYM...

A: Most days, apart from when you have reformer Pilates, but then you try and squeeze in some extra cardio at 6am
B: When you know you're going to be in a bathing suit
C: Never

14. MAKEUP IS...

A: Your life
B: A lifesaver when you're hungover
C: A guilty secret

15. YOU HAVE SEX...

A: When your date buys you dinner
B: When you feel like it
C: Once a month on a Saturday night at 10.15pm and pre-brunch on a Sunday

HOW DID YOU DO?

MOSTLY AS
You are: **Coreless**
Sorry to break it to you, but you're basically basic. Bet you don't even own a fleece.

MOSTLY BS
You are: **Midcore**
You like dipping your toe into the trend but you're not fully ready to commit.

MOSTLY CS
You are: **Borecore**
You're hardcore, maybe try relaxing once in a while, like in your sleep or something?

INDEX

ACKNOWLEDGMENTS

Thanks to Flush, the very non-Normcore cockapoo, for sitting on my lap the whole time I wrote this. Thus ensuring it took at least double the time.

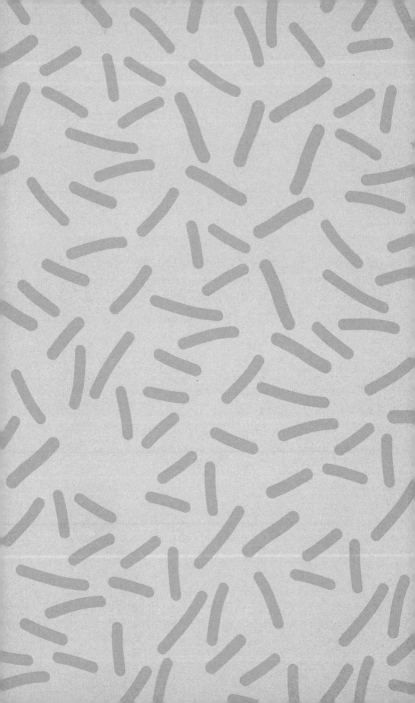